ideals EASTER

More Than 50 Years of Celebrating Life's Most Treasured Moments

Vol. 52, No. 2

"The promise of resurrection is written on every leaf that grows."
—*Author Unknown*

IDEALS—Vol. 52, No. 2 March MCMXCV IDEALS (ISSN 0019-137X) is published eight times a year: February, March, May, June, August, September, November, December by IDEALS PUBLICATIONS INCORPORATED, 565 Marriott Drive, Suite 800, Nashville, TN 37214. Second-class postage paid at Nashville, Tennessee, and additional mailing offices. Copyright © MCMXCV by IDEALS PUBLICATIONS INCORPORATED. POSTMASTER: Send address changes to Ideals, PO Box 148000, Nashville, TN 37214-8000. All rights reserved. Title IDEALS registered U.S. Patent Office.

SINGLE ISSUE—U.S. $4.95; Higher in Canada
ONE-YEAR SUBSCRIPTION—8 issues—U.S. $19.95 USD; Canada $36.00 CDN (incl. GST and shipping); Foreign $25.95 USD
TWO-YEAR SUBSCRIPTION—16 issues—U.S. $35.95 USD; Canada $66.50 CDN (incl. GST and shipping); Foreign $47.95 USD

Printed and bound in USA by The Banta Company, Menasha, Wisconsin. Printed on Weyerhaeuser Husky.

The paper used in this publication meets the minimum requirements of
American National Standard for Information Sciences—Permanence of Paper for Printed Library Materials, ANSI Z39.48-1984.

Unsolicited manuscripts will not be returned without a self-addressed, stamped envelope.

ISBN 0-8249-1124-5

Cover Photo
EASTER BOUQUET
Norman Poole Photography

Inside Front Cover
GIRL WITH RABBIT
From the collection of Thomas L. Cathey
under license of Sunrise Publications Inc.

Inside Back Cover
VICTORIAN CHILD
Sunrise Publications Inc.

Easter

M. Donnaleen Howitt

The world is waking up again,
    Its winter sleep is done.
The leaves shake out their pale green folds
    And dry them in the sun.

A crocus pushes through the earth
    And stretches from her sleep;
A robin trots across the grass,
    His springtime date to keep.

The lambs and chicks and baby ducks
    Explore each lovely thing;
The pussywillows pop their husks,
    And butterflies take wing.

At Easter all the world is fresh,
    The dismal days are through;
Each living thing is born again,
    And all the dreams are new.

BROOKGREEN GARDENS
Murrells Inlet, South Carolina
William Johnson
Johnson's Photography

The Lowly Crocus

Esther K. Haarstad

The wind came whistling round my door—
    A sudden gust, then a roar.
    Why do you sing so loud a song?
    Why do you prattle all day long?

Broken branches scattered near;
    Fallen leaves, drab and drear,
    Lay lifeless by the garden wall.
    How I wished for spring to call!

But March was teasing me to play—
The sun shone bright and clear one day.
    I pulled my jacket on and then
    Tucked a scarf about my chin.

A flash of purple caught my eye,
Close to the ground, beneath the sky—

Such a small and tender bloom!
It chased away my ling'ring gloom.

How could a crocus be so bold
To rise and face the chilling cold?
Then greet me with a happy smile,
    Bringing gladness all the while.

Tell me, now, who cared for you
When the wind blew and blew?
How could your petals safely last
    During such a stormy blast?

He who shields a lowly flower
    Surely cares for me each hour.
    So I will rest secure tonight
And greet the morning shining bright.

Opposite Page
FIRST CROCUSES
Ina Mackey

Border
CLOSE-UP CROCUSES
Adam Jones

ECHO IN TIME

J. A. Giunta

A craggy bluff beneath my feet,
The winds about my frame,
Buffeting rock and cloth replete—
A force no one can tame.

Into the gale I raise my voice,
A cry to eons past;
Eternal song of ageless choice
For years unto the last.

A solemn winter heeds my call
With calming, sodden skies—
A melody in nature's hall
To welcome spring's arise.

OWL CLOVER AND POPPIES
Organ Pipe Cactus National Monument
Arizona
Bob Clemenz Photography

When April Comes

Beverly J. Anderson

Such joy is ours when April comes
    And all the earth is new.
The hills are gowned in green once more;
    The skies are fairest blue.

The scent of lilacs fills the air
    And rides on gentle breeze,
And robins sing in symphony
    From yonder cherry trees.

The daffodils are wearing frills,
    The dogwood's dressed in lace,
And violets from shady nooks
    Peer out with purple face.

How beautiful Your world, O Lord,
    When April comes to bless
Our hearts and lives with renewed hope
    And springtime happiness.

9

Readers' Reflections

How Great Thou Art

The sun appeared in the eastern sky
As I arose to greet the dawn.
The sky was aflame with color
As a brand new day was born.
The grass was sparkling with morning dew;
The fragrance of flowers filled the air.
Birds were singing their songs of praise;
Joy and beauty seemed everywhere.
I gazed on the scene around me;
Joy and gladness filled my heart,
As I softly whispered to myself,
"Dear Lord my God how great Thou art."

Peggy Gaarde
Murphys, California

Welcome to Spring

We look forward to your annual coming;
We welcome you wondrous Spring.
We're awed by your warmth and beauty,
And the uplifting gifts you bring.

With fragrant and colorful flowers,
Vegetables and fruits galore,
Songbirds, waterfalls, warm, balmy nights—

How could we ask for more?
We love your sibling seasons—
Summer, Winter, and Fall—
But you stand for life and glorious rebirt
So perhaps you're the best of all!

Jack G. Robb
Chowchilla, Californ

Spring's Promise

As winter's cold and darkness lingers,
The bulbs beneath poke up their fingers.
They test the air for any sign
Of weather that might be benign.

The tiny snowdrop pops up first
To tell us winter's past is worst.
The crocus next, with colors blazing,
Greets our winter window-gazing.

With colors like an Easter treat
Come hyacinths with fragrance sweet.
The daffodil and tulip too
Delight us with their vibrant hue.

Magnolia, dogwood, cherry, quince
Fill barren twigs with blossoms dense.
Like flags of promise these appear;
The winter's gone and spring is here.

Donna Jean Paterson
Portland, Oregon

Spring

Vibrant hues of pink and yellow
Arise from the remains of winter chills—
The end of hot cocoa and tracks in the snow,
The beginning of blue crocuses and daffodils.

The scent of a new season is breaking through
The blanket of frost strewn on our front lawn.
The dogwood blooms to a sky so blue
As the birds begin to sing at the crack of dawn.

Time for daytime to overcome nighttime
And for children to romp around outside.
So many kites to fly and trees to climb;
Millions of budding bushes give places to hide.

Pastel sundresses and sky-high sunflowers,
Dangling toes in a cool, shallow river,
Easter egg hunts and April showers
Remove the brisk and icy winter shiver.

Stephanie Chamberlin
Mount Holly, New Jersey

Editor's Note: Readers are invited to submit unpublished, original poetry for possible publication in future issues of Ideals. Please send copies only; manuscripts will not be returned. Writers receive $10 for each published submission. Send material to Readers' Reflections, Ideals Publications Inc., P.O. Box 148000, Nashville, TN 37214-8000.

Spring Blossoms

Bonnie Lee Swain

Her face looked familiar, but I couldn't quite place the visitor until she introduced herself as the daughter of Mrs. Lucidi, my across-the-street neighbor. Gina Allen, a businesswoman, was direct and to the point. "I hate to impose, but I need to ask a favor. You probably know that Mother is home-bound. I check on her twice a week to see that she's all right, and Senior Volunteers bring her lunch daily." I nodded, thinking that was about all I knew of Mrs. Lucidi. Gina explained that she would be working in another state for four months and her mother did not require a nurse. "But there is no one to make sure that she hasn't fallen and broken something, forgotten to order fuel, and so on. Would you mind checking on her every few days?"

"I'd be glad to. In fact, I can take her dinner," I offered.

"No, that's not necessary, thank you."

I assured Gina that it would be a pleasure. The next day I walked over to Mrs. Lucidi's after lunch to formally introduce myself. I had lived in the apartment across from her for two months. I missed the roomy house I'd left, but the small apartment was all I could afford for now. What I missed most of all was my yard. I loved flowers, especially daffodils and hyacinths. I couldn't bring my bulbs to the apartment because the front was too shady and the sunnier back was used for parking.

When Mrs. Lucidi finally came to her door, her hair was uncombed and she wore a robe. Perhaps he'd been in bed, I thought. I introduced myself, explained that I'd promised Gina to keep an eye on her mother, and asked if I could do anything.

"No," she said gruffly. "Thank-a you. I know Gina ask you to come-a over here. I am okay. Goodbye now." Mrs. Lucidi had a heavy Italian accent and was obviously not pleased to have a visitor. Still, I had promised Gina. I vowed to myself that I would at least try again in a few days.

Meanwhile, I began paying more attention to Mrs. Lucidi's small, neat house. Her yard grew a nice carpet of grass, but there were no flowers. Of course, it was early winter, not the season to see many flowers. Occasionally I saw Mrs. Lucidi peek through her blinds, but otherwise she never made an appearance.

The next time I went to see her, Saturday afternoon, she was again wearing her robe. But on this very cold day she surprised me by inviting me in—sort of. "Come. It is cold. You fix-a the heat for me?" I showed her how to operate the wall thermostat. "Okay. Thank-a you," was her only response.

As winter progressed, we continued our routine. I knocked, Mrs. Lucidi answered, said she was fine, thank you, and goodbye. How boring it must be for her now! But she still seemed not to want company.

One afternoon as I walked back to my apartment after receiving the usual greeting from Mrs. Lucidi, I stopped in her front yard. I noticed for the first time how sunny it was. Suddenly it dawned on me that she might let me plant bulbs in her front yard for both of us to enjoy! I turned back to ask her.

"Bulbs? What bulbs? Light bulbs?" she asked.

"No, flower bulbs. See?" I showed her the catalog of hyacinths, daffodils, tulips, and anemones that I kept in my pocketbook. "They're simple to care for and don't even take a lot of digging. But they do need sun, and I have no place to plant them."

She shrugged magnificently, as only Old World Italians can do, and turned away. "You plant," she gave in, disinterested.

It was late to plant bulbs, but the ground wasn't yet frozen, so I purchased an assortment of bulbs I knew to be strong and good producers—hyacinths, brightly colored and fragrant, and several types of tulips. Finally, the daffodils. Large buttercup yellow ones, delicate pale ones with ruffled centers, and my favorite, geranium daffodils, which grow several white flowers with orange centers on each stem and

have a strong, very sweet fragrance. I caught Mrs. Lucidi peeking out the window several times to watch me plant them.

The next week she asked me, "How long? The flower bulbs, how long to grow?" I explained that the hyacinths and daffodils would be up first in March. One week later, she asked to see the pictures again. I left my catalog with her, with the ones I'd planted marked. When she returned the well-worn catalog the next week, she confided, "In the town where I was born, we had flowers like some of these. Very pretty flowers."

By the second week in February, I noticed Mrs. Lucidi putting her blinds up early in the morning, and sometimes I even saw her looking out the window at the flower beds. Now, when I went over to visit, I carefully checked the beds. I was eager to spot the first sprout breaking ground so I could tell her. Soon the day came. She was at the door before I knocked. "One is growing?" she asked, excited. "Yes, yes," I assured her. "They'll all be growing soon."

The next day I saw her blinds up, and she was pacing back and forth in her living room. I hurried over to see what was wrong. She asked if I would take her out to see the flower. She was even dressed to go out, for the first time since I'd met her! I was delighted to help her down the steps and over to the tiny cracks in the half-frozen ground where the greenish-white nose of a hyacinth peeked out. She looked at it awhile, pronounced it *bene* (good), and returned to the warmth of the house. I helped her in and stayed only a few minutes. She was still quiet, and tired, but she looked younger somehow.

Over the next few weeks as more flowers poked up through the cold gray dirt, Mrs. Lucidi was blooming too. She began to come outside almost every day to check on the flowers' progress. By the time the buds were ready to open, she was up early every morning, dressed, and walking carefully with a cane in her pretty little yard. As gorgeous as those first hyacinths and daffodils were, they couldn't compare with the "roses" in Mrs. Lucidi's cheeks when visiting "my" flowers in the cool spring air.

When Gina came home she could hardly believe the transformation in her mother. With my blessings, of course, Mrs. Lucidi talked Gina into taking her and some fresh-cut flowers to visit a friend. And the other day I heard Mrs. Lucidi say, "Gina! Let's go buy flower bulbs. You plant, I smell!"

"Who loves a garden, loves a greenhouse too." —*William Cowper*

THE GREENHOUSE

Craig E. Sathoff

The greenhouse is a thrilling place
    Each season of the year,
But I especially like it
    When spring at last is here.

The little boxes row on row
    Of seedlings to be set
Provide the surest sign of spring
    That I have noticed yet.

Tomatoes, phlox, and cabbages
    And pansies, deepest blue,
And pepper plants and broccoli
    Are waiting for me too.

It's really rather hard to choose
    The plant that I like best,
For each is lovely in its way
    And different from the rest.

Petunias that I always plant
    Along my garden way
Are there in every size and shape
    And color bright and gay.

It always fills my heart with joy
    And makes my spirits sing
To visit at the greenhouse shop
    When spring is blossoming.

From My Garden Journal

by Deana Deck

THE EGG TREE

Have you noticed that people seem to do more holiday decorating than they used to? It's a cheerful trend. In our neighborhood, "egg trees" greet the Easter holiday festooned with plastic eggs dangling from colored ribbons. It's very festive and contributes to a sense of community.

If you're not up to decorating the yard, there's another, even more interesting way to enjoy an Easter "egg tree," but you'll have to wait until next year to enjoy it.

It was just prior to the Easter holidays one year that I first learned about this kind of egg tree. I edit a question-and-answer garden column for the local Sunday paper, and when a reader inquired about obtaining an egg tree plant in time for Easter, I was mystified. The description was intriguing—colored eggs on a living plant—but I could find no information anywhere. I gave up and admitted failure to my readers, inviting anyone who knew anything of the plant to please share the information.

Not long after that I received a photocopied article from an old magazine which included photographs of the plant and (Eureka!) a botanical name. The mystery plant, which I had decided must be a genetically engineered wonder of science, turned out to be simply a variety of the common garden eggplant. But what a variety! Since the article listed a source for seeds, I immediately sent away for a pack and, armed with a proper Latin name, set about learning all I could.

The egg tree (*Solanum melongena*) belongs to the same huge family as tomatoes and potatoes. Some members of this family, like the Bitter Nightshade, are poisonous, but the fruit of the egg tree, like the familiar eggplant, is not only edible, but quite delectable. A native of Thailand, the egg tree is grown for food in many countries, primarily in the Middle East and in Mediterranean regions.

While solving the mystery of the egg tree, I also unraveled another mystery. I have always loved the smooth surface and deep color of a ripe eggplant. It's a color that seed catalogs refer to as purple, although I consider that a poor description for that rich shade that the French so eloquently call *aubergine*. The mystery that had haunted me since I first encountered an eggplant on my mother's kitchen counter was why it bore that name.

It looked like no egg I'd ever seen. It was big and purple. Eggs were little and white. The contradiction nagged at me for years until, while researching the egg tree, I discovered the answer: the egg—egg tree, that is—came first. Its garden variety cousin was named in its honor, not the other way around.

The egg tree is a small, shrublike plant that produces fruit exactly the same size and shape as a hen's egg. When the fruits first appear, they are white. As they mature, they turn yellow, then rich gold in color. Like a contented hen, the plant will keep producing "eggs" as long as the growing conditions are right. Eventually, it can bear purple blossoms and "eggs" of white and various shades of yellow and gold all at once.

If the fruit is picked as soon as it is fully ripe, a mature plant will continue to produce for much of the year in the proper environment. Unfortunately, the proper environment is tropical. In the temperate zones of the United States, you can start it indoors from seed in January, use it as an Easter centerpiece in March or April, then move it outdoors for the summer. While it's possible to nurse it through the winter, it seems like a lot of bother, unless you live in Florida. The egg tree has a fairly short life span of about three years, and the plants are so easy to grow from seed that I just abandon them in fall.

Provide your egg tree with warm soil, plenty of sun, good fertilizer, and a consistent but not overly-generous supply of water. Since it needs temperatures of 75°F or higher to germinate, a perfect spot to start one is on a south-facing window sill, in a greenhouse, or on a sun porch. While the seedlings are sprouting, spray the soil daily with water to keep the seeds slightly moist, but not soggy. Once they sprout, water from below by setting the containers on a gravel-filled tray of water. Avoid over-watering.

I start the seeds in small peat pots that can be planted into a larger container later without disturbing the roots. When the plants have outgrown their baby beds, put them in ten-inch pots and you won't have to move them again. Even as seedlings, egg trees send out a fairly deep root system, so dig carefully if you don't use peat pots.

Use a rich soil mixture of one-third garden soil, one-third peat moss (to retain moisture), and one-third sand or perlite (to encourage drainage). Before adding the plants, mix a time-release fertilizer into the soil. As with all heavy producers, the egg tree will use up a lot of soil nutrients in a very short time. If you do not amend the soil with fertilizer when transplanting, be sure to feed weekly with a well-balanced plant food high in phosphates.

It will take about two months for your plant to bloom and three to begin producing fruit, so time your planting accordingly if an Easter egg tree is your goal. To make up for the shorter days of late winter and early spring, it's a good idea to position a horticultural grow light over the plants. I just keep mine on a timer so that it comes on around dusk and goes off about 10:00 p.m. As the days begin to lengthen, I adjust the timer accordingly.

The first fruits will appear when the blossoms drop off. They will look like little white peas at first, but will soon grow to the size of hens' eggs. As they mature they will begin to change color. Remove ripe fruit to extend the growing season and discourage the plant from going to seed.

Time the plant's move to the patio or porch about the same time you put your houseplants out. Wait until night temperatures are consistently in the 65°F to 70°F range.

This plant's usefulness extends far beyond its duties as a holiday decoration. Harvest fruit can be used in many recipes, just like the ordinary eggplant. In order to grow your own, you'll need seeds from a catalog the first time, but you can save your own for subsequent crops since the plant has not been hybridized. Search your catalogs carefully. Most list the plant as an eggplant variety in the vegetable section, but some list it in the flower seed section as the Easter Eggplant.

If you have the space to grow more than one, pot several as gifts. They make great Easter morning surprises for children, and adults will be equally delighted.

Deana Deck lives in Nashville, Tennessee, where her popular garden column is a regular feature in The Tennessean.

A Prayer for Henry

Evelyn Bence

Last evening I stood
and watched old Henry
plant his garden.
Like a boy in a dirt pile
he dug valleys,
made them rivers;
built mountains,
pushed them flat.

With those earth-moving hands
he set a year in motion:
burying seeds
to harvest
a bushel of life.

He's done this so often,
three score and more springs,
in faith that he'll pick
the fruit in its season.

Lord, grant him
an eternity of summers,
sunshine to ripen
the fruit of his spirit.

Country CHRONICLE
Lansing Christman

I am always aware of the beauty of nature blossoming in the spring, but this year at Eastertime I was particularly struck by the lovely pinks and golds throughout the countryside of South Carolina. They were everywhere—in the yards, in the fields, and by the roadsides. The pink of the peach orchards represented to me my dawn, the youth of time, the rich beginning. Turning to some nearby fields, I smiled to see the masses of gold in the wild mustard flowers, acres of them shining in the light of the sun. Those golden blooms reminded me of the process of aging.

Here was the pink of the peach trees in full bloom, the blossoms a sunrise pink. This was my morning. The golden heads of the mustard resembled the glow of late afternoon as the day prepared for its sunset, so appropriate and so symbolic of the cycle of life.

I have gone through both stages, both youth and age. I have experienced the joy of watching the year bring out its blooms, so much like the spring of life. Then the gold of the wild mustard, turning field after field into masses of golden hues that to me, at least, brought to mind my golden years.

There they were, the pink bringing to mind my own youth, the tenderness, the beginning. Then I thought of those fields of gold as symbolic of age, making me, at eighty-five, more at peace with myself and the world, giving me a contentment that all is well now that I am among the elderly, facing the same sunset of life that I am facing, remembering that beyond the sunset will be another dawn, for God has said that he who believes will have eternal life. The resurrection puts peace in my soul.

The fresh, lovely pink of the peach trees, the wild mustard's gold. The sunrise, the sunset—the young, the old.

The author of two published books, Lansing Christman has been contributing to Ideals for over twenty years. Mr. Christman has also been published in several American, foreign, and braille anthologies. He lives in rural South Carolina.

PEACH ORCHARD AND WILD MUSTARD
Willamette Valley, Oregon
Steve Terrill Photography

Whenever I See Lilacs Blow

Edna Jaques

Whenever I see lilacs blow
My heart rejoices and I know
That in a world far off, somewhere,
There is a God who answers prayer.

Whenever I see lilacs bloom
After the winter's cold and gloom,
Something within, deep down inside
Tells me that all good things abide.

Whenever I see lilacs tall
Growing against a garden wall
My faith is strengthened and renewed
And I am filled with gratitude.

Beyond these little grief hung years
Above anxiety and tears,
There's something bigger than it all,
Someone who hears me when I call.

All these eternal things I know
Whenever I see lilacs blow.

COMMON LILACS
orton Arboretum
sle, Illinois
ichael Shedlock

Handmade Heirloom

Mary Skarmeas

DECOUPAGE FLOWER POTS. Pots crafted by Lisa Thompson. Jerry Koser Photography.

DECOUPAGE FLOWER POTS

By combining the traditional elements of an age-old art with modern techniques, new materials, and your own unique style, you can create one-of-a kind decoupage heirlooms that will add warmth and cheer to any home.

Decoupage has its roots in the Orient. When the Venetian explorer Marco Polo opened the seaway to the Far East, he also opened the eyes of Europeans to the many wonders of the Orient, one of which was its beautiful lacquered furniture. Chinese artists hand-painted tables, chairs, armoires, and screens with bucolic scenes and then covered their meticulous works of art with at least twenty coats of transparent lacquer. The results were elegant, high-glossed pieces of furniture, which by the seventeenth century had caught the eyes and won the hearts of the Italian people. Due to its unique beauty, authentic Chinese lacquered furniture commanded a high price in Polo's native land; and because of the expense and difficulty of shipping items from the Far East, the furniture was also quite rare and considered a symbol of great status.

The Venetians, however, were undaunted by these obstacles. They wanted the look of fine hand-painted Chinese lacquered furniture in their homes and were determined to have it. Inspired by the skilled Chinese artisans, they applied a little cunning ingenuity and creative deception to create their own version of Chinese lacquer ware. The Venetian version of the craft became known as *lacca povera*, which translates as "poor man's lacquer." Decorative, pre-printed paper replaced the hours of hand-painting; and, instead of twenty coats of Chinese lacquer, the Venetians got by with a few coats of varnish, just enough to create the illusion of hand-painted decorations under high-gloss lacquer.

With this Venetian innovation, it was not long before the art of cutting and pasting paper and sealing it to furniture with varnish became popular all over Europe. It was in France that the new craft became known as *decoupage*, which translates literally as "a cutting out."

Decoupage was embraced by professional craftspeople and hobbyists alike. At a time when intricately painted furniture was the height of fashion, decoupage offered an opportunity to all classes of people to have at least the illusion of the latest in home decor. The craft hit its peak of popularity in the eighteenth century when Marie Antoinette, queen of France, joined the craze, commissioning paintings by famous artists to be cut up and varnished onto furniture by the queen and her ladies-in-waiting. The decoupage fad spread throughout Europe and to the United States before a change in the preferred style of furniture from painted to carved led the interests of craftspeople elsewhere.

Today we may have little interest in decoupaging our furniture, but the techniques of the centuries-old craft, updated with modern materials and methods, can be very attractive. Twenty coats of lacquer have been replaced by three coats of spray-on polyurethane, and choices of paper are virtually unlimited—colored and printed tissue, gift-wrap, greeting cards, calendar prints, wallpaper, hand-made paper, children's drawings, and anything else that is appealing or meaningful to the craftsperson.

The aim of decoupage is to create the illusion of hand-painting. Thanks to the innovations of the Venetians centuries ago, we too can create this illusion with some pretty paper, a bit of glue, and the magic of clear-drying varnish. Modern decoupage transforms everyday household objects into lovely works of art with true heirloom potential.

Decoupage has been liberated from large, heavy pieces of furniture. Today, almost any solid surface is suitable for decoupage. Simple clay flower pots are a good place to start if you are new to the craft. They offer not only a good surface for decoupaging, but for those interested in crafts with lasting appeal they are also a practical item that will always find a place in our homes. Choose whatever size clay pot suits your needs. Try one with a matching saucer for an extra touch of class. For paper, buy some pretty floral napkins—the only requirement is that they be at least two-ply. Cut off the textured edges of the napkin and peel off the top layer from as many napkins as needed to cover the inside and outside surfaces of the pot and its saucer.

Cover your work table with waxed paper. Beginning on the outside of the pot, brush a light coat of a clear drying glue to the pot one small section at a time, immediately applying one piece of napkin to each section. To give the pot a finished look, continue the napkins over the rim and under the base, stopping short of the drainage hole. Press the paper onto the glue, letting the paper wrinkle for an interesting effect. Continue in the same fashion until the pot and saucer are completely covered. Let the pots dry thoroughly before spraying with three coats of clear gloss varnish, drying between each coat according to the directions on can.

The flower pots that result from these simple steps recall the work of the Venetian imitators who, through simple means, created elegant furniture in the tradition of the finest Chinese craftspeople. Beneath the varnish, the simple paper napkin takes on the look of fine hand-painted lacquer ware. Finished pots can serve as elegant gift boxes to be filled with appropriate goodies for any special occasion. Of course, the pots will also hold any plant or flower you choose. Take some bright blossoms to a sick friend or a new neighbor, or say "Happy Easter" with a special plant.

Your decoupage flower pot will become a wonderful heirloom gift with a little extra work. Take a cutting from one of your own cherished plants and start the new plant in your decoupage pot. The result is a gift with true continuity—perfect for a new baby, a wedding, or a special anniversary. In this way, decoupage is no longer an art of imitation but an original expression from your heart.

Mary Skarmeas lives in Danvers, Massachusetts, and is studying for her bachelor's degree in English at Suffolk University. Mother of four and grandmother of one, Mary loves all crafts, especially knitting.

BITS & PIECES

I want a row of hollyhocks
Across my garden there,
And several rows of crimson phlox;
And, if there's room to spare,
A little clump of bleeding hearts,
Old-fashioned though they be,
And lots and lots of four-o'clocks
To tell the time for me!
MYRTLE VORST SHEPPARD

They speak of hope to the fainting heart;
With a voice of promise they come and part.
They sleep in dust through the wintry hours;
They break forth in glory—bring flowers, bright flowers!
MRS. HEMANS

I think of the garden after the rain,
And hope to my heart comes singing.
At morn the cherry blooms will be white,
And the Easter bells be ringing!
EDNA DEAN PROCTER

26

Flowers are the poetry of earth,
as stars are the poetry of heaven.
AUTHOR UNKNOWN

The sun is bright, the air is clear,
The darting swallows soar and sing,
And from the stately elms I hear
The bluebird prophesying spring.
HENRY WADSWORTH LONGFELLOW

Let patience grow in your garden.
AUTHOR UNKNOWN

My garden is a place of love;
Each tender plant a thought divinely born.
GRACE MATHEWS WALKER

lowers preach to us if we will hear.
CHRISTINA G. ROSSETTI

As for marigolds, poppies, hollyhocks,
and valorous sunflowers, we shall never
have a garden without them, both for
their own sake, and for the sake of old-
fashioned folks, who used to love them.
HENRY WARD BEECHER

27

In the Garden

C. Austin Miles

I come to the garden alone,
While the dew is still on the roses;
 And the voice I hear,
 Falling on my ear,
The Son of God discloses.

Chorus
And He walks with me,
And He talks with me,
And He tells me I am His own;
 And the joy we share
 As we tarry there,
None other has ever known.

He speaks, and the sound of His voice
Is so sweet the birds hush their singing;
 And the melody
 That He gave to me,
Within my heart is ringing.

I'd stay in the garden with Him,
Though the night around me be falling,
 But He bids me go;
 Through the voice of woe
His voice to me is calling.

McCLAY STATE GARDENS
Tallahassee, Florida
Ian Adams Photography

The Little Church

Jane Mullenax

I passed a little church today
Its doors were open wide
Bidding me welcome, saying
Come, come inside.

Slowly I retraced my steps,
Climbed the threshold floor.
All the while I asked myself,
What am I here for?

Suddenly a ray of sun flashed
Across the gloom.
It was there and then I knew
God was in that room.

In that quiet, awesome silence
Of that room that lay so bare
I heard a voice say softly,
"Child, I am with you everywhere."

THROUGH MY WINDOW

Pamela Kennedy
Art by Russ Flint

EASTER 101

Teaching first and second graders in Sunday School is an inspiring, if sometimes daunting, proposition. A child of six or seven years has that dangerous mix of knowledge, experience, and spontaneity that brings unexpected interpretations to the most ordinary situations. When confronted with the great events and teachings of Scripture, these little believers often bring fresh insights that give new life to even the mustiest passages.

I recall teaching a lesson on the Creation to a group of children one morning. After explaining how God spoke the different elements of the universe into existence, one particularly impressed little fellow raised his hand and asked, "No lasers, no magic words, no nothing?" I said he had pretty well summed up the whole situation. "Wow," he added. "That beats Superman!"

When my own son came home from his class one Sunday, carrying a crayon drawing of two men and a dog warming themselves by a fire, I asked him about the day's lesson.

"Well," he replied, pointing to the figures in the picture, "these are those guys at the fiery furnace."

"Weren't there three guys?" I questioned, recalling Shadrach, Meshach, and Abednego, thrown into the fire by an angry Persian king.

"No, Mom," he patiently explained. "There was Shadrach and Meshach, and a pet named Go!"

Although I have often had doubts about the amount of real theology dispensed in my class, one Easter I was given a lesson I'll never forget.

Searching for a way to make the different elements of the Easter story real to my young students, I decided to allow them to take part in the preparation of the lesson. On Palm Sunday,

I gave each child a hollow plastic egg. "Next week," I said, "I want each of you to bring back your egg with something inside that reminds you of Easter; then we will talk about all the things we have brought in to share."

The class was an interesting mix of youngsters. We had quiet and vocal ones, rambunctious ones, and those who preferred to sit and draw pictures quietly. But my biggest challenge that year was a little boy named Marty. Marty had satiny black hair and big brown eyes that darted around the room as if he were expecting to see something frightening any minute. He often refused to take part in activities and his papers were rarely completed. But the thing that bothered me most about Marty was that he hardly ever spoke. It was difficult to gauge his understanding, and I was convinced he was getting nothing out of Sunday School class although he was there most Sundays. His mother assured me, "Marty loves Sunday School." But I figured she was just being polite.

After I handed out the plastic eggs, I showed the children how they came apart in the middle and repeated the instructions. "Does everyone understand?" I asked. Little heads nodded back at me. "Marty?" I inquired. Startled, the brown eyes raised, then lowered quickly. He nodded slowly as he pushed the halves of his egg back together. I sighed as the children left that day and wondered what I could do to reach little Marty with God's love.

On Easter Sunday, the children tumbled into the classroom, resplendent in ruffles and floral prints, miniature suits and clip-on ties. They eagerly placed their colored plastic eggs in the basket I had positioned in the story circle. I was glad to see Marty drop his egg in with the others and wondered what he had brought to share.

After a few minutes of welcome activities, we moved to the chairs grouped around the basket. One by one the children came to open their eggs and share their symbols of Easter. One girl brought a tiny chick made of yarn; another brought a candy egg. Thomas, my class clown, produced a coiled-up pipe cleaner and informed us, "It's because Easter is in the SPRING! Get it?" He collapsed on the floor, laughing hysterically at his own wit.

Having recovered from Thomas's offering, we continued around the group. It seemed that most of the children had forgotten about the religious significance of the holiday, and I was feeling like a failure as a teacher until Sarah produced a little metal cross and we were able to get into the more spiritual side of things.

Finally, there was one egg left and I looked at Marty. "Would you like to open your egg for us, Marty?" He shook his head.

"How about if I open it for you? I'm sure everyone is looking forward to seeing what you brought." He looked up at me shyly and gave a little nod.

Carefully, I pulled apart the blue egg. Nothing fell out. I tipped the halves and peered in. There was nothing stuck inside.

"Marty didn't bring nothin'!" observed one of the boys. Some of the others giggled.

My mind was racing. How could I spare this sensitive child the embarrassment he was obviously experiencing? "Marty, is there something you'd like to share about your egg?" I asked, grasping at a possible way out.

Tentatively, Marty got out of his chair and came to my side. He took the two halves of the blue plastic egg and then walked over to the big picture in the center of our bulletin board. In a small, but clear voice, he said to the children:

"I *didn't* bring nothin', I brought Easter."

My eyes filled with tears as I saw the truth Marty alone had understood; for over his head on the bulletin board was a picture of the empty tomb.

Pamela Kennedy is a freelance writer of short stories, articles, essays, and children's books. Wife of a naval officer and mother of three children, she has made her home on both U.S. coasts and currently resides in Honolulu, Hawaii. She draws her material from her own experiences and memories, adding highlights from her imagination to add to the story.

Easter Morning

Kay Hoffman

I watched a lily from the barren sod
Lift up a pure white bloom to God;
A robin came at break of dawn
And sang his joyous morning song.

Sweet blossom scent, like incense rare,
Imbued the dew-drenched morning air;
The soft pink mist of dawn made way
For the sun's first golden ray.

On a hillside near so lately bare
A dogwood tree bloomed wondrous fair;
God had the springtime world adorned
For this His resurrection morn.

Easter Prayer

Kay Hoffman

Once again it's Easter morning
And joyous church bells ring;
"Christ, Our Lord, is risen!"
The white-robed choirs sing.

The Easter message is retold
As it has been before —
How the angels rolled away the stone
From the tomb's dark door.

Our hearts are joined in one accord
As now we humbly pray:
"From our heart's door this Easter morn,
Lord, roll the stone away."

The Last Supper

And when the hour was come, he sat down, and the twelve apostles with him.

And he said unto them, With desire I have desired to eat this passover with you before I suffer:

For I say unto you, I will not any more eat thereof, until it be fulfilled in the kingdom of God.

And he took the cup, and gave thanks, and said, Take this, and divide it among yourselves:

For I say unto you, I will not drink of the fruit of the vine, until the kingdom of God shall come.

And he took bread, and gave thanks, and brake it, and gave unto them, saying, This is my body which is given for you: this do in remembrance of me.

Likewise also the cup after supper, saying, This cup is the new testament in my blood, which is shed for you.

Luke 22: 14-20

In 1308, the great artist Duccio created the high altar of the Duomo in Siena, Italy; hence, the Maesta. Forty-six of the original fifty-eight fresco panels survive today and are displayed in the Museo dell'Opera Metropolitana in Siena. The Maesta was the zenith of Duccio's artistic career and is his only remaining documented work.

THE LAST SUPPER
Duccio, Maesta
Museo dell'Opera Metropolitana
Siena, Italy
Scala/Art Resource, New York

In the Garden

Then cometh Jesus with them unto a place called Gethsemane, and saith unto the disciples, Sit ye here, while I go and pray yonder.

And he took with him Peter and the two sons of Zebedee, and began to be sorrowful and very heavy.

Then saith he unto them, My soul is exceeding sorrowful, even unto death: tarry ye here, and watch with me.

And he went a little further, and fell on his face, and prayed, saying, O my Father, if it be possible, let this cup pass from me: nevertheless not as I will, but as thou wilt.

And he cometh unto the disciples, and findeth them asleep, and saith unto Peter, What, could ye not watch with me one hour? Watch and pray, that ye enter not into temptation: the spirit indeed is willing, but the flesh is weak.

He went away again the second time, and prayed, saying, O my Father, if this cup may not pass away from me, except I drink it, thy will be done.

And he came and found them asleep again: for their eyes were heavy. And he left them, and went away again, and prayed the third time, saying the same words.

MATTHEW 26: 36–44

AGONY IN THE GARDEN
Duccio, Maesta
Museo dell'Opera Metropolitana
Siena, Italy
Scala/Art Resource, New York

The Betrayal

And while he yet spake, behold a multitude, and he that was called Judas, one of the twelve, went before them, and drew near unto Jesus to kiss him.

But Jesus said unto him, Judas, betrayest thou the Son of man with a kiss?

When they which were about him saw what would follow, they said unto him, Lord, shall we smite with the sword?

And one of them smote the servant of the high priest, and cut off his right ear.

And Jesus answered and said, Suffer ye thus far. And he touched his ear, and healed him.

Then Jesus said unto the chief priests, and captains of the temple, and the elders, which were come to him, Be ye come out, as against a thief, with swords and staves?

When I was daily with you in the temple, ye stretched forth no hands against me: but this is your hour, and the power of darkness.

Luke 22: 47–53

KISS OF JUDAS
Duccio, Maesta
Museo dell'Opera Metropolitana
Siena, Italy
Scala/Art Resource, New York

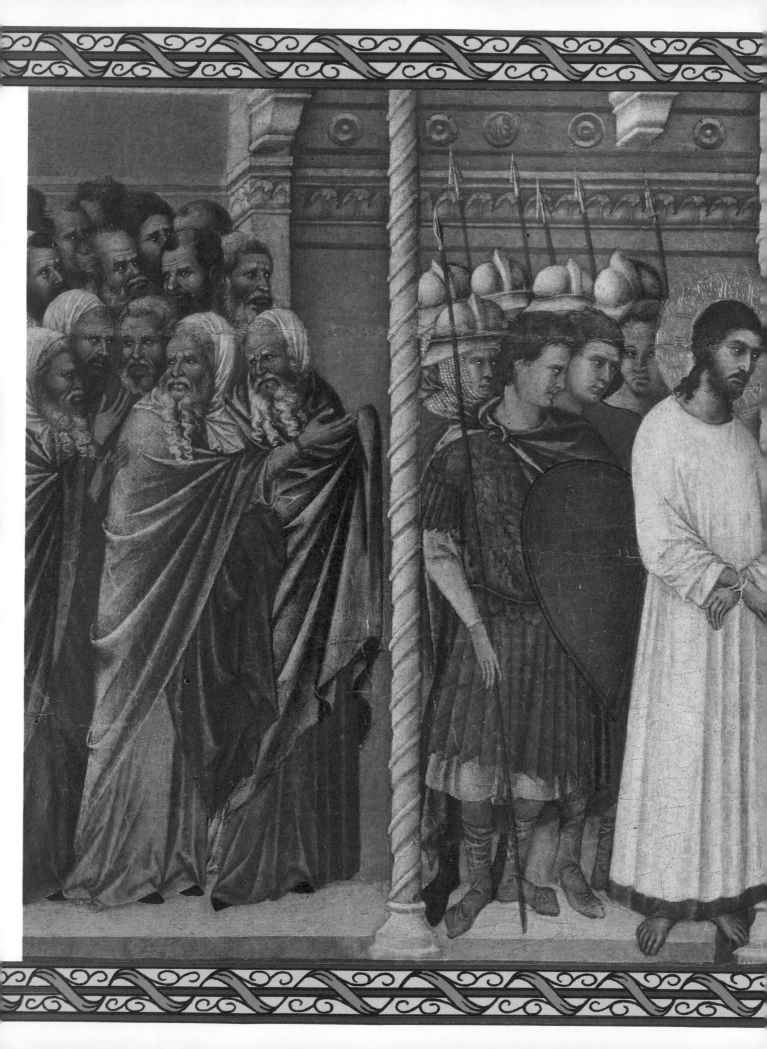

Christ before Pilate

And straightway in the morning the chief priests held a consultation with the elders and scribes and the whole council, and bound Jesus, and carried him away, and delivered him to Pilate.

And Pilate asked him, Art thou the King of the Jews? And he answering said unto him, Thou sayest it. And the chief priests accused him of many things: but he answered nothing. And Pilate asked him again, saying, Answerest thou nothing? behold how many things they witness against thee. But Jesus yet answered nothing; so that Pilate marvelled.

And the multitude crying aloud began to desire him to do as he had ever done unto them.

But Pilate answered them, saying, Will ye that I release unto you the King of the Jews? But the chief priests moved the people, that he should rather release Barabbas unto them. And Pilate answered and said again unto them, What will ye then that I shall do unto him whom ye call the King of the Jews?

And they cried out again, Crucify him.

MARK 15: 1-5, 8-9, 11-13

The Son of God

And Jesus cried with a loud voice, and gave up the ghost.

And the veil of the temple was rent in twain from the top to the bottom. And when the centurion, which stood over against him, saw that he so cried out, and gave up the ghost, he said, Truly this man was the Son of God.

There were also women looking on afar off: among whom was Mary Magdalene, and Mary the mother of James the less and of Joses, and Salome;

And now when the even was come, because it was the preparation, that is, the day before the sabbath,

Joseph of Arimathaea, an honourable counsellor, which also waited for the kingdom of God, came, and went in boldly unto Pilate, and craved the body of Jesus.

And Pilate marvelled if he were already dead: and calling unto him the centurion, he asked him whether he had been any while dead. And when he knew it of the centurion, he gave the body to Joseph.

And he bought fine linen, and took him down, and wrapped him in the linen, and laid him in a sepulchre which was hewn out of a rock, and rolled a stone unto the door of the sepulchre.

Mark 15: 37-40; 42-46

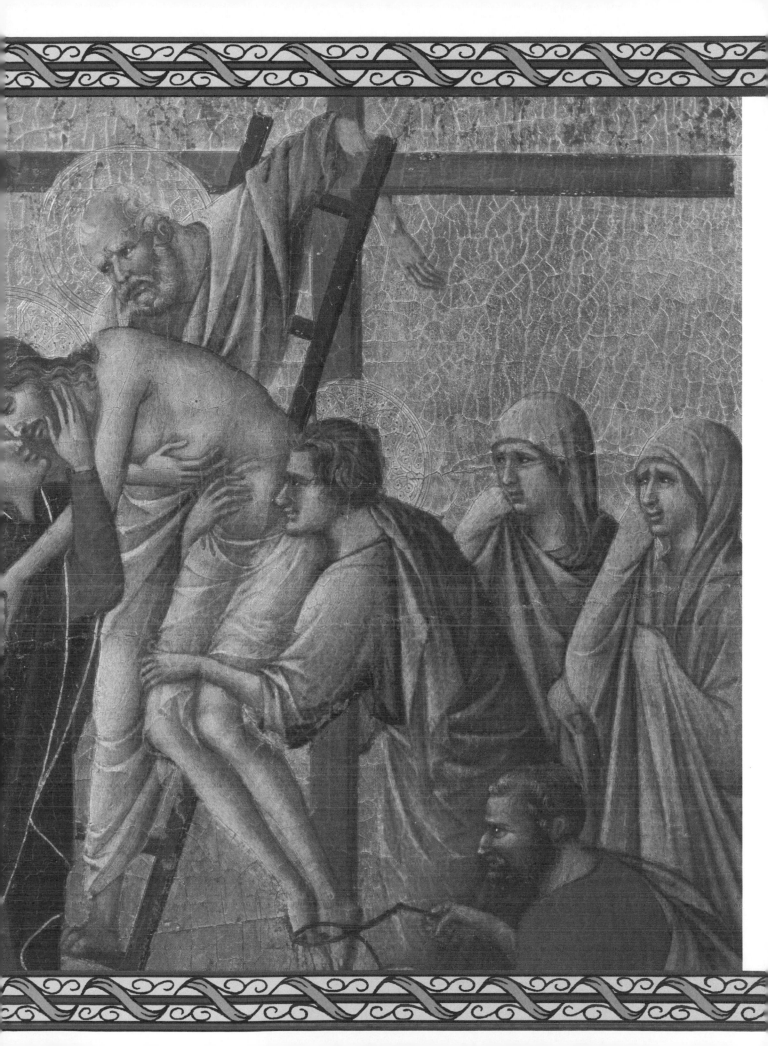

The Open Tomb

And, behold, there was a great earthquake: for the angel of the Lord descended from heaven, and came and rolled back the stone from the door, and sat upon it.

His countenance was like lightning, and his raiment white as snow:

And for fear of him the keepers did shake, and became as dead men.

And the angel answered and said unto the women, Fear not ye: for I know that ye seek Jesus, which was crucified.

He is not here: for he is risen, as he said. Come, see the place where the Lord lay. And go quickly, and tell his disciples that he is risen from the dead; and, behold, he goeth before you into Galilee; there shall ye see him: lo, I have told you.

And they departed quickly from the sepulchre with fear and great joy; and did run to bring his disciples word.

MATTHEW 28: 2–8

THE THREE MARYS AT THE TOMB
Duccio, Maesta
Museo dell'Opera Metropolitana
Siena, Italy
Scala/Art Resource, New York

The Appearance to Mary

But Mary stood without at the sepulchre weeping: and as she wept, she stooped down, and looked into the sepulchre,

And seeth two angels in white sitting, the one at the head, and the other at the feet, where the body of Jesus had lain.

And they say unto her, Woman, why weepest thou? She saith unto them, Because they have taken away my Lord, and I know not where they have laid him.

And when she had thus said, she turned herself back, and saw Jesus standing, and knew not that it was Jesus.

Jesus saith unto her, Woman, why weepest thou? whom seekest thou? She, supposing him to be the gardener, saith unto him, Sir, if thou have borne him hence, tell me where thou hast laid him, and I will take him away.

Jesus saith unto her, Mary. She turned herself, and saith unto him, Rabboni; which is to say, Master.

Jesus saith unto her, Touch me not; for I am not yet ascended to my Father: but go to my brethren, and say unto them, I ascend unto my Father, and your Father; and to my God, and your God.

JOHN 20: 11–17

NOLI ME TANGERE
Duccio, Maesta
Museo dell'Opera Metropolitana
Siena, Italy
Scala/Art Resource, New York

The Resurrection

Jonathan Henderson Brooks

His friends went off and left Him dead
In Joseph's subterranean bed,
Embalmed with myrrh and sweet aloes,
And wrapped in snow-white burial clothes.

Then shrewd men came and set a seal
Upon His grave, lest thieves should steal
His lifeless form away and claim
For Him an undeserving fame.

"There is no use," the soldiers said,
"Of standing sentries by the dead."
Wherefore, they drew their cloaks around
Themselves, and fell upon the ground,

And slept like dead men, all night through,
In the pale moonlight and chilling dew.

A muffled whiff of sudden breath
Ruffled the passive air of death.

He woke, and raised Himself in bed;
Recalled how He was crucified;
Touched both hands' fingers to His head,
And lightly felt His fresh-healed side.

Then with a deep, triumphant sigh,
He cooly put His grace-clothes by—
Folded the sweet, white winding sheet,
The toweling, the linen bands,
The napkin, all with careful hands—
And left the borrowed chamber neat.

His steps were like the breaking day:
So soft across the watch He stole,
He did not wake a single soul,
Nor spill one dewdrop by the way.

Now Calvary was loveliness:
Lilies that flowered thereupon
Pulled of the white moon's pallid dress,
And put the morning's vesture on.

"Why seek the living among the dead?
He is not here," the angel said.

The early winds took up the words,
And bore them to the lilting birds,
The leafing trees and everything
That breathed the living breath of Spring.

Mary Magdalene

Paula Haase

She stands beside the empty tomb
  As soon as it is day,
And none can penetrate the gloom
  Or wipe her tears away,
For He, who brought Life to her soul,
  Forgiving all her sin,
Whose very Word had made her whole,
  Was laid to rest within.

But now she finds that hollow room
  All bleak and bare inside;
Oh who would dare to disentomb
  That holy One Who died?
And who could be that soulless wretch
  So lacking in respect
As to commit such sacrilege,
  So craven and abject?

And so she stands beside the tomb,
  The essence of despair,
Enveloped in such heartsick gloom
  That she is not aware
That He, Whom she so deeply mourns,
  Is standing by her side,
Still wearing the imprint of thorns,
  His nail-scarred hands flung wide.

He speaks, transforming into joy
  The sorrow of her heart,
And none can evermore destroy
  The peace which He imparts.
Thus hastening to spread the word
  To saddened hearts that weep,
She glories in her risen Lord,
  Her joy ecstatic, deep.

LEGENDARY AMERICANS

Nancy Skarmeas

RACHEL CARSON
Marine Biologist and Writer

As a student at the Pennsylvania College for Women in the 1920s, Rachel Carson faced the most difficult decision of her life. She had come to the school on scholarship as an English major with dreams of becoming a writer. Since the age of ten she had written stories, first for *St. Nicholas* magazine and later for school papers. In an age when women were rarely encouraged to seek careers outside the home, Carson had her heart set on becoming an author.

But she had another dream. Since she was a young girl, Carson—the child of western Pennsylvania farmers—had dreamed of studying the sea. Her biology classes renewed those dreams and filled her mind with a new career ambition. Mid-

way through her college years, she changed her major from English to biology. It was an agonizing decision for Carson, who believed that in choosing to follow the path of the biologist she was abandoning forever her dreams of becoming a writer.

As she immersed herself in the study of marine biology, writing seemed a part of her past. Upon graduation, she received two remarkable opportunities. First, she was offered a summer position at the Woods Hole ocean research center in Massachusetts. Not only was this a wonderful opportunity at a respected center, but it was also the fulfillment of her childhood dream—she would finally see the ocean. Second, Carson went from Woods Hole to Johns Hopkins University in Baltimore to study for her master's degree.

While at Johns Hopkins, Carson not only kept up her studies while fighting the prejudices against women in higher education, but she also worked at two part-time jobs to support herself and her elderly parents. When Rachel Carson earned her master's degree in marine biology in 1932, she had achieved something truly remarkable; but she still faced overwhelming odds as she entered the job market. The Depression made any work hard to come by, and most men in her field were skeptical of women's ability. But Carson left no room for doubt. She took the civil service exam for fisheries biologists—the only woman to do so—and received the highest score.

With her degree and her test score in hand, she applied at the United States Bureau of Fisheries and was hired. But it was not the job she had hoped for. Budgets were tight, and what the Bureau of Fisheries needed was someone with a knowledge of marine biology who also possessed writing skills, someone who could put together the department's books and pamphlets and make the technical world of science understandable to the average American. Rachel Carson began her career in marine biology not as a biologist in the field but as a writer.

By changing her major to biology and pursuing her dreams of the sea, Carson had not abandoned her dream of becoming a writer after all. At the Department of Fisheries, her two dreams came together in a wonderful way. Asked to write a brief introduction for a pamphlet about fish, Carson wrote an essay about the beauty and balance of life in the sea—an essay her supervisor told her was too good for a pamphlet and should be sent to *The Atlantic Monthly* magazine. Carson did not take his words seriously until later when—supporting by then not only her widowed mother but also two orphaned nieces—she sent in her article to *The Atlantic* in hopes of extra money. The article caught the attention of editors who believed it good enough to be a book. In 1941, Carson's first book, *Under the Sea Wind*, was published. It combined scientific knowledge with accessible, compelling language to create a text that scientists and non-scientists alike could appreciate. Carson's message was simple yet vital: all life in the sea is tied together in one beautifully balanced system.

The pattern of Carson's career was now set. The more she studied the sea, the more she was inspired to write and share her knowledge with the world. And the more she worked on organizing her research for her writing, the more she understood the important larger picture revealed by her studies. The tools of the marine biologist allowed her to study the intricate workings of sea life; the skills of the writer allowed her to transform those details into a unified vision to present to the world.

Carson's second book, *The Sea Around Us*, described the perfect, wasteless ecological balance of sea life. At a time when words like "ecology," "pollution," and "conservation" were not part of the American vocabulary, Carson described how nature is inherently, delicately balanced and how the ecology of the sea echoes and complements the ecology of all the earth. *The Sea Around Us* became a best seller and was hailed by critics as both scientifically accurate and poetically written.

Carson's third book, *The Edge of the Sea*, expanded her area of study to life forms on the eastern sea coast. Again, her message was a broad one—life on the edge of the sea has its own system of balance and ecology, which is intermingled with that of the sea and the land, and in which every life form plays a part. Through Carson's writing, people began to see their natural world in a different light.

Carson's greatest impact came with her last book, written as she struggled with the cancer that would end her life before she reached the age of sixty. *Silent Spring* was inspired by the deaths of fourteen robins on a friend's property after the spraying of the pesticide DDT. Horrified by this destruction of life, Carson launched her own study into DDT. The results were frightening and were met with denial from the pesticide industry and disbelief from the American public, who wanted to believe that the government protected them from such harm. Carson's message was now more urgent. "Man is a part of Nature," Carson said in an interview after the publication of *Silent Spring*, "and his war against Nature is . . . a war against himself." For years Carson had been writing about the delicate ecological balance of life in the sea and along the shore. Now her message was in the form of a warning. The spraying of DDT—meant to kill insects—had led to the death of the robins: its effect on humans and the rest of the ecosystem was still to be discovered.

Silent Spring was published in 1962. Its impact was far-reaching. President John F. Kennedy responded to Carson's book by creating a commission to study the use of pesticides. Although Rachel Carson died in 1964, her book continued to influence the country. In 1970, the Environmental Protection Agency was formed, and by 1972, the EPA had outlawed the sale and use of DDT.

As a young girl, Rachel Carson dreamed of the sea—a faraway, magical place to a girl in western Pennsylvania. She also dreamed of becoming a writer. What she never could have dreamed, however, is that her two great passions would one day combine to enlighten the world to the wonders of the sea, to the delicate balance of nature, and to the responsibility of humans to respect the environment. Rachel Carson gave up her plans for a life of writing to pursue other dreams only to discover that to be a successful writer is not only to be skilled with words, but to use that skill to carry a message to the world. The story of her life is an inspiration, a reminder to us all that the secret to leaving one's mark upon the world lies in the dreams we hold nearest our hearts.

Life

Thelma Lee Cottrell

I watch the ocean day by day,
And see the little wavelets play,
Chasing each other in the sun,
Like happy children having fun.

Sometimes the water's smooth, serene,
Hardly a ripple to be seen.
At other times, it's dark and gray,
Warning a storm is on the way.

Soon the winds howl, the waters roar
And mighty torrents lash the shore.

But when morning dawns at last,
The terror of the night is past.
Flowers, fresh washed; the grass so green
And all the world seems bright and clean.

How much like life, it seems to me,
This changing picture of the sea.
Sometimes our lives are bright and gay
And simple pleasures fill our day.

Then suddenly all this is past.
The storm's upon us! We're aghast
At its might and fury. Our spirits quail,
Our courage falters in the gale.

But finally through morning haze
We lift to heaven our feeble gaze.
The day brings hope! The storm departs!
And God speaks peace unto our hearts.

WHITETAIL DEER. Rachel Carson National Wildlife Refuge, Maine. Bill Silliker Jr. Photography.

RACHEL CARSON NATIONAL WILDLIFE REFUGE
Wells, Maine

The Rachel Carson National Wildlife Refuge embraces forty-five miles of the most beautiful coastal wetlands in Maine. Named for legendary environmental writer and marine biologist Rachel Carson, the refuge is a magical place where life on land meets life in the sea.

The dynamic ecosystem that thrives at the Rachel Carson National Wildlife Refuge is sustained by an unusual phenomenon in Maine—

a salt marsh. Salt marshes are fragile environmental communities that develop in areas where the waves of the ocean slow to gentle ripples, and a plant called cordgrass takes root and builds a marsh. The dense meadows at the marsh's edges, the meandering tidal creeks which flood and drain the marsh twice a day, and the ponds of salt, called salt pans, all rely on the salt marsh for sustenance.

The salt pans are an especially interesting aspect of the refuge. These are small, ponded areas that develop when the low areas of the marsh hold salt water as the tide recedes. When the water evaporates, salt is concentrated in the pans, which support plants such as glassworts and sea blite as well as small invertebrate animals. The salt pans are important feeding areas for waterfowl and shorebirds.

One section of the refuge, called Hemlock Hollow, features an evergreen woodland of mostly hemlocks and white pines. Even though the evergreens are out of sight of the marsh, they are directly linked to it. Ground water in the woodland carries nutrients from the decaying leaves and needles to the marsh. Many of the refuge's mammals and birds rely on both the marsh and the woodland for food and breeding habitat.

This valuable combination of sea and land provides habitats for a wide variety of birds, mammals, and plants, including several federal and state endangered and threatened species: the peregrine falcon, the roseate tern, the bald eagle, the piping plover, and the least tern. The refuge also provides habitats for mammals such as deer, moose, otter, and fox. Plants typical of both northern and southern forests are found in the refuge, which results in a spectacular array of plant species in a single locale.

The refuge is divided into ten areas that lie in nine different communities. The headquarters for the refuge is in Wells, Maine. Most of the refuge can be viewed from public roads, but for those nature lovers who want a more personal experience, the Rachel Carson Trail offers a one-mile interpretive walk along an upland edge where striking vistas and close-up encounters alike can be enjoyed. The trail is accessible for persons with disabilities.

The Rachel Carson National Wildlife Refuge, administered by the U.S. Fish and Wildlife Service, is exactly what the name states: a safe haven for wildlife. The area is not, therefore, a highly developed park full of recreational areas and picnic shelters but rather a protected area in which visitors have the opportunity to view wildlife and learn more about conservation and preservation.

Formerly called the Coastal Maine Seacoast Refuge, the Rachel Carson National Wildlife Refuge was renamed in 1969, five years after her death, to commemorate her accomplishments. Renaming the refuge pays homage to an extraordinary woman who worked for the U.S. Fish and Wildlife Service from 1936 to 1952, first as a biologist, then as a writer and editor. The region was well-known by Carson, who spent her summers on Southport Island and conducted research in the area for several of her books. The careful preservation of this beloved area is a tribute to her study and dedication.

> *"It is a wholesome and necessary thing for us to turn again to the earth and in the contemplation of her beauties to know the sense of wonder and humility."*
>
> —*Rachel Carson*

Messenger

Sister Clarasine Bahleda

A little bird this morning
   Flew by my window pane.
He circled all around the yard
   And then came back again.

He perched upon my window sill
   And cocked a saucy eye.
"Madame," he sang, "are you aware
   That Lady Spring is nigh?

"Just see the grass a-greening
   And newborn buds stretch out
Their tiny, fragile, baby heads
   To see what the world's about.

"Jonquils, first to brave the frost,
   Lift high their golden heads,

While purple-petaled crocuses
   Peer out from winter beds.

"I hear an eager, tumbling brook,
   Escaped from ice-bound shell
Softly murmuring to itself
   Alive to springtime's spell.

"Small forest creatures, born again,
   Frolic among the trees,
Chattering their joy for all to hear,
   Loving the warm, soft breeze.

"So don't sit there dreaming!
   Madame, the world is *new!*
Come out and taste the freshness."
   And off to the skies he flew.

The bluebird carries the sky on his back.
—Henry David Thoreau

COLLECTOR'S CORNER

Layne Cameron

PURPLE MARTIN HOUSE. Jean Higgins, New England Stock Photo.

BIRDHOUSES

House hunting is a universal dilemma. Just as we humans visit many different homes to find the perfect dwelling, the same is true for our feathered friends. Happily, birds today are becoming overwhelmed with the selection of quality homes from which to choose. Some still want the simplicity of a one-door, basic birdhouse, others are moving into upscale, gingerbread-covered, miniature Victorian mansions or modern, multi-story apartment buildings.

Birds are drawn in by the shape and size of the opening hole and the placement of the house in the yard. Even the color will affect which species will make a birdhouse home. Most birds are looking for homes in neutral tones of dull brown, green, or gray in which to

start a family. The purple martin, in contrast, is more interested in interior temperature, which is why it prefers a white home that will reflect heat from the sun.

While collectors are looking for many of these same features, they are looking for much more and sometimes are willing to pay top dollar for quality birdhouses, both old and new.

American pioneers began building birdhouses as a way to attract insect-eating birds that would protect their crops. During the winters, when field work was at a minimum, creative craftspeople built miniature models of the town church or their own barn. In New York City during the 1850s, craftsmen built elaborate birdhouses as scaled-down versions of the mansions they accompanied. Soon hous-

62

ing for the bird population became a popular folk art. Today, birds and collectors alike enjoy everything from simple craft designs to architecturally drafted birdhouses.

America's top architects have accepted the challenge to build modern birdhouses that have the same qualities we look for in our own homes. A classic revival villa designed by Robert Stern, complete with white columns and a copper roof, can sell for several thousand dollars. Famous architects' houses aside, most collectors agree that sales in that range are rare. But the precedent has been set, and collectors are flocking to galleries and countryside shops looking for the perfect find. A martin mansion farmhouse from the 1950s recently sold in the thousand-dollar range. Accented with a silo, three chimneys, shingles, and windows and doors that could be opened and closed, its accessibility and solid construction were valued by both birds and collectors.

A worthwhile discovery for the antique collector would be an authentic, older birdhouse with a lived-in feel. Marks from beak sharpening, foot traffic, and irregular wear and fade in the paint are strong indicators of authenticity. For example, paint should be less faded under the eaves than the more exposed areas. Maybe a shutter has a slight crack or is hanging slightly cockeyed. A sharp eye will detect attempts to repair a house's imperfections. Upkeep can actually diminish the value of a collectible birdhouse.

This increase in demand has brought some collectors to say birdhouse collecting is in its golden age, and some collectors believe the gloaming of this golden age has arrived. The reason is simple: Most of the old birdhouses have been bought and they are not being resold. New-found interest in collecting birdhouses has inspired a number of builders.

Some collectors label new homes as impostors. Others believe that some builders of the new birdhouses exhibit an attention to detail and a reverence for tradition that makes the houses worth waiting a year or more to get. Peggy Sperry of Jamesport, Missouri, is one such builder. Each of her houses is inspired by a unique building. It may be something she sees in a photograph from one of her customers, or it may be an old lighthouse seen during one of her excursions across the country. Whatever the inspiration, Peggy makes some sketches and returns to her shop. Her next step is to find a dilapidated house from which she can gather the wood that provides the weathered texture she treasures. Peggy picks up shingles, nails, stones, and anything else she can recycle. The final touch is a coat of rich buttermilk-based paint that Peggy mixes herself in order to achieve the subtle shades of red and mustard she desires.

After exhausting the antique stores and estate sales, collectors look to builders such as Peggy to feed their collections. Nostalgic collectors will sometimes attempt to recreate their hometowns or vacation villages, while others focus on specific buildings, such as churches or firehouses.

The age-old argument of birdhousing is how to properly display a collection. Purists believe, with the support of the bird community, that birdhouses are meant to hang from trees, accent gardens, or perch high atop posts to provide housing for birds. The joy of sighting a family of tree swallows, sparrows, or martins raising their young is the true mission for these collectors. The opposition argues that such beautiful creations should not suffer the beating of an outdoor environment. They believe these houses are too fragile to handle the rigors of winter and should be pampered and displayed above mantels or brought out only as holiday decorations. Still others cross party lines and have houses lining bookshelves as well as hanging from trees.

No matter how the collections are displayed, the demand for this folk art rivals the success experienced by decoys and weather vanes. Birdhouses can be spotted in country antique shops, craft shows, flea markets, and even galleries of primitive art. Perhaps they'll soon be spotted in your garden or on your mantel, and you'll know what experienced collectors know: Birdhouses are not just for the birds.

House Hunting

Rosa Larson

Two little birds
In the tree up above,
They must be newlyweds;
They are so much in love.

He likes the place,
The price is right;
She thinks thick leaves
Will shut out the light.

So, they fly off together
In a huff, I can see.
I hope for domestic bliss
And a family in my tree.

Message

Jane Smallwood

The message I've been
expecting
came today
delivered to the house
by a tiny field mouse
so dainty, so gay
twittering in passing
"Spring's on the way!"

NATURAL LOG BIRDHOUSE
IN CHERRY TREE
Missouri
Gay Bumgarne

MORNING MIST ON THE FARM. A. Devaney, Inc., New York.

INVENTIONS BLOSSOM ON THE FARM

Farmers who like to tinker, and others who do it from plain necessity because fix-it shops don't lie around the corner, are doing a fine job these days at meeting wartime machinery shortages. "Jitterbug tractors" have been rigged up from old auto parts and other junk retrieved from scrap heaps.

Homemade weed cutters that, Charlie McCarthy-like, "mow 'em down!"; post-hole diggers; tractor-powered wood saws; a "lift wagon" that handily dumps corn into a truck without scooping—these and countless other contrivances, including a cow-tail holder that makes milking easier, have been "thought up" by the farmers themselves.

From north, south, east, and west—from Illinois, North Dakota, Ohio, New York, Washington,

Idaho, and Oklahoma—come stories of the farmers' ingenuity.

And farm folks are sharing their ideas. Farmers like to share, and do, though their next-door neighbors may live a mile away, with no trolley or bus line moving past the door to make neighboring easy.

North Dakota farmers have had a sort of sharing society for the past thirty-seven years in an organization called the Northwest Farm Managers' Association. One of its many projects has been this very thing of passing along ideas about homemade machinery and gadgets.

In Illinois recently, farmers swapped such labor-saving ideas in a series of traveling exhibits or fairs that the University of Illinois' Extension Division took from county to county.

Many of the inventions shown in Illinois were so simple and effective that farmers went directly from the exhibitions to blacksmith shops, it's said, to see about having similar devices made ready for their use by the time spring work started.

An old washing machine motor, in one instance, was used to power a weed cutter mounted between two bicycle wheels. Its owner designed it particularly for use along fence rows and claimed it would "mow down weeds as thick as broomsticks."

Though corn harvest time in the Middle West was a long way off, with spring not yet arrived, Illinois farmers paid a lot of attention to the "lift wagon" that W. W. Sentel of Sullivan, Illinois, fixed up. He designed it to lessen the labor and time it takes to scoop corn from a wagon into a truck when the corn is hauled from the field. Mr. Sentel doesn't have to scoop his now. His corn picker throws the yellow ears into his lift wagon at the wagon's normal height. When the wagon is full, he elevates the box from the frame, a hinged door or gate at one end of the box tips down—and presto!—the corn shoots down into the waiting truck.

There was a homemade elevator for baled hay exhibited by Alvin Rentschler of Chestnut, Illinois. A half horsepower electric motor operated the moving chains and their cleats, which carried bales of hay from wagons up into the barn lot. It's common practice thereabouts to save labor in haymaking by using a field pick-up baler—loading the bales immediately into a rack wagon, and hauling them at once to the barn or other storage.

Erwin Gehlback of Lincoln, Illinois, showed how he made a feed truck. He mounted a sixty-bushel hopper tank and an elevator on an old truck and used it to haul feed to fill the self-feeders on his 255-acre stock farm.

George Gehlback, also of Lincoln, Illinois, who raises turkeys, made a three-horsepower tractor from an old engine and auto parts. He calls it a "chore tractor" and says with it he hauls feed and water to pigs out in pasture. And when he takes the cart off, the tractor can be run between corn rows, or used for seeding rye for pasture. He can also attach his lawn mower to it.

From up in North Dakota, from Oklahoma, Ohio, and New York, come stories of "jitterbug tractors" rigged up from this and that since new ones couldn't be obtained from mail-order catalogues.

In Ohio, it is related, a handy garage mechanic boasted to farmers that he could make them jitterbug tractors for $100 apiece—that he could make them out of old truck parts. He did, and then the farmers went to work and built jitterbug tractors themselves. While this homemade model doesn't pretend to do the heavy work a general tractor can do, it does many lighter chores—mows and rakes hay, pulls the corn binder, sows oats and wheat, and plows the garden.

In Oklahoma, a farmer made a tractor with forty-eight speed combinations out of two old trucks. It cost him $175.

Rigging up homemade machinery and other equipment on farms has been given a lot of attention by the Northwest Farm Managers' Association since it was first formed—away back when North Dakota was a real frontier and buffalo still roamed the prairies, says Cap E. Miller, its secretary-treasurer. Many a farmer had to invent his own equipment in those days, if he was to have any. And now North Dakota farmers are at it again.

The present-day "roll-in method" of putting hay in barns was perfected by one of the Association's members a long time ago, Cap Miller states. This farmer knocked a rack-wide hole in the front of his barn, backed up his loaded hay wagon, and with ropes rolled the hay right in.

A more recent North Dakota farm invention is a one-man tractor-driven post-hole digger made from $20 worth of used parts, including an old Dodge rear-end assembly.

Completed, the post-hole digger was fastened to the front of a tractor. It will dig a half mile of holes thirty-six inches deep and twenty feet apart in about six hours.

Detailed instructions about how to make the post-hole digger, and countless other labor-saving farm devices made by the Association's members are on file in its offices at Fargo, North Dakota.

The University of Illinois also plans to make available complete instructions for rigging up the best inventions found during its recent county show meanderings.

Originally printed in The Christian Science Monitor Magazine, *April 21, 1945.*

A SLICE OF LIFE

Edgar A. Guest

The White Oak

The white oak keeps it leaves till spring
   when other trees are bare,
And who will take the time to look,
   will find the young bud there;
The young bud nestled snug and warm
   against the winter's cold;
The young bud being sheltered
   by the knowledge of the old.

And when the spring shall come again—
    and gentle turns the day,
The youthful bud will swell with strength
    and thrust the old away;
The youthful bud will seek the breeze
    and hunger for the sun,
And down to earth will fall the old
    with all its duty done.

Then, heedless of the parent leaf,
    the youthful bud will grow
And watch the robins build their nests
    and watch the robins go.
Then something strange will come to it
    when that young leaf grows old,
It too will want to shield its babe
    against the winter's cold.

It too will cling unto the tree
    through many a dreary day
Until the springtime comes again
    and it is thrust away;
Then it will flutter down to earth
    with all its duty done,
And leave behind its happy child
    to drink the morning sun.

How like man's life from birth to close!
    How like the white oak tree
Which keeps a shelter for its young
    against the storms, are we!
We guard our children through the night
    and watch them through the day,
And when at last our work is done,
    like leaves, we fall away.

Edgar A. Guest began his illustrious career in 1895 at the age of fourteen when his work first appeared in the Detroit Free Press. His column was syndicated in over 300 newspapers, and he became known as "The Poet of the People."

April Song for a Small Child

Maxine Jennings

Race with me, child, to the greening hill
When sun creeps over the steep incline
Toward fragile gold of daffodil
Where fledgling grass looks up to pine.
The creek's full rhythm and the fine
Lyrics that early robins sing
Are treasures to keep should storms combine
When the year has carried you
    far from spring.

Morning in pink and petaled chill
Has fashioned an opalescent shrine
With frosty prism and crystal frill
And mauve-gold mist at the borderline

Where sun and shadow intertwine.
See how the ice-jeweled branches swing!
Remember, child, this blithe design
When the year has carried you
    far from spring.

Note how the sky spreads warmth until
Reluctant patches of snow decline
And hasten toward meadows, rill on rill,
In a filigree like a silver vine.
The leafy laughter of wind is sign
That joy is a bright, forever thing.
Let clouds repeat their rainbow shine
When the year has carried you
    far from spring.

AN EASTER HUG
Pam Sharp
New England Stock Photo

FOR THE CHILDREN
ARTWORK BY RUSS FLINT

APRIL RAIN SONG
Langston Hughes

Let the rain kiss you.
Let the rain beat upon your head with silver
    liquid drops.
Let the rain sing you a lullaby.

The rain makes still pools on the sidewalk.
The rain makes running pools in the gutter.
The rain plays a little sleep-song on our roof
    at night—

And I love the rain.

---

*The unique perspective of Russ Flint's artistic style has
made him a favorite of* Ideals *readers for many years. A
resident of California and father of four, Russ Flint has
illustrated a children's Bible and many other books.*

Bride

Elsie B. Block

Bride of the night, my cherry tree
Stands in simple dignity,
Erect and waiting, while the moon
Points out the blossoms gently strewn
Before her path, the pebbled way
That winds to where the waters play
From fairy fountains' trembling tunes
Of sweetest strain. All afternoons
Seem far less lovely than this night
Made breathless by the bridal white.

CHERRY TREE BLOSSOMS
Amherst, New Hampshire
William Johnson
Johnson's Photography

Ideals' Family Recipes

Favorite Recipes from the Ideals Family of Readers

Editor's Note: Please send us your best-loved recipes! Mail a typed copy of the recipe along with your name, address, and telephone number to Ideals magazine, ATTN: Recipes, P.O. Box 148000, Nashville, Tennessee 37214-8000. We will pay $10 for each recipe used. Recipes cannot be returned.

An Easter Brunch

CHEESE ROLL-UPS

In a mixing bowl, combine two 8-ounce packages softened cream cheese, ½ cup granulated sugar, and 2 egg yolks. Cream until fluffy; set aside.

In a separate mixing bowl, combine 1 cup granulated sugar and 1 teaspoon cinnamon; mix well. Set aside.

Remove the crusts from 1½ loaves square sandwich bread. Roll each slice flat with a rolling pin. Spread about 2 tablespoons cream cheese filling on each bread slice; roll up jelly-roll fashion. Brush rolls with melted butter and sprinkle with cinnamon-sugar mixture. Cut rolls in half and place seam-side down on an ungreased cookie sheet. Continue for remaining bread slices. Bake in a preheated 350° oven for 15 minutes.

Mildred Drahokoupil
Berwyn, Illinois

CREAMY AU GRATIN POTATOES AND HAM

In a medium saucepan, cover ¾ cup diced onion with water; simmer until tender. Drain. In a large mixing bowl, combine the cooked onion, one 32-ounce package frozen hash brown potatoes, one 10¾-ounce can cream of celery soup, ⅔ cup shredded Cheddar cheese, and 2 cups diced ham. Add salt and pepper to taste. Pour ingredients into a greased 9- x 13-inch baking dish; cover with foil. Bake in a preheated 350° oven for 45 minutes or until potatoes are tender.

Bev Dennison
Fostoria, Ohio

MAKE-AHEAD BREAKFAST BAKE

In a large skillet, crumble one 1-pound package breakfast sausage. Cook over medium heat until well done; drain on paper towels. Set aside.

Slice off crusts of 4 slices of sandwich bread; cut into cubes. Spread cubes in the bottom of a buttered 9- x 13-inch baking dish. Top with cooked sausage and 2 cups shredded sharp Cheddar cheese. Set aside.

In a mixing bowl, combine 6 beaten eggs, ½ teaspoon salt, and 2 cups milk. Pour over cheese and sausage. Cover and refrigerate overnight. Bake uncovered in a preheated 350° oven for 30 to 40 minutes. Serves 12 to 14.

Norma Neel
Belmont, North Carolina

DELIGHTFUL MACEDONIA

In a large mixing bowl, combine 2 peeled, seeded, and cubed pears; 2 peeled, pitted, and cubed peaches; 2 peeled and sliced bananas; 10 maraschino cherries, halved; 18 seedless purple grapes; 6 tangerine sections, halved; 1 cup pineapple chunks; and ¼ cup powdered sugar. Mix well and chill. To serve, place fruit in sherbet glasses, top with vanilla ice cream and whipped topping.

Iolan Carroll
Marietta, Georgia

Readers' Forum

Meet Our Ideals Readers and Their Families

KITTY PULLIAM of Trenton, Tennessee, sent us this charming shot of her great-granddaughter Hannah Grace Carroll, baby daughter of Amy and Kevin Carroll of Mt. Juliet, Tennessee, and granddaughter of Tommy and Carol Pulliam of Houston, Texas. Hannah is ready for St. Patrick's Day in her green, clover-leaf sunglasses. Kitty says Hannah is "one of the most beautiful babies in the whole world." And we're sure that is Great-Grandma's completely unbiased opinion!

Kitty works at the Accent House interior decorating and gift shop in Trenton, where they sell *Ideals* magazine on a regular basis. Shoppers in Trenton be warned: a certain proud great-grandmother may buy up all of the *Ideals Valentine* issues herself!

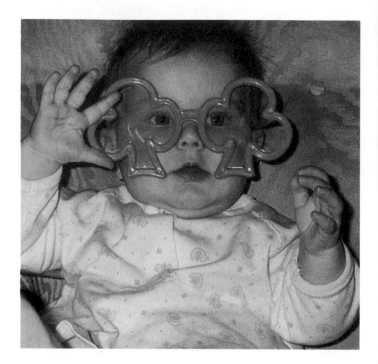

FRANCES FULTON, of West Creek, New Jersey, has seen many pets achieve "star" status in our Readers' Forum, so she decided to send us this photo of Muffin in action. Muffin was adopted by Frances and her husband John after her mother was discovered in the backyard nursing three baby kittens. The Fultons found good homes for two of the kittens and kept Muffin for themselves.

Frances and John have four children and thirteen grandchildren who live throughout the United States. Frances keeps busy with Muffin, her craftwork, and her love for the outdoors.

MARILYN BRUECK of Kissimmee, Florida, couldn't decide if she should send us the photograph of her granddaughter Erin displaying her "usual sunny disposition, or the one in which she tells the world that she has posed for one too many pictures in her Easter finery," so she sent both! Erin is the daughter of Molly and Kevin Murphy and lives in White Bear Lake, Minnesota.

The six children of Marilyn and her husband Joe have blessed their parents with fourteen grandchildren ranging in ages from one to eighteen. Even though the family is scattered throughout the state of Florida and the Midwest, everyone remains close via frequent telephone calls and visits. Also, Marilyn and Joe's home is popular as the site of family vacations due to its proximity to the many Florida attractions and the beach!

THANK YOU Kitty Pulliam, Frances Fulton, and Marilyn Brueck for sharing with *Ideals* in this Easter issue. We hope to hear from other readers who would like to share photos and stories with the *Ideals* family. Please include a self-addressed, stamped envelope if you would like the photos returned. Keep your original photographs for safekeeping and send duplicate photos along with your name, address, and telephone number to:

Readers' Forum
Ideals Publications Inc.
P.O. Box 148000
Nashville, TN 37214-8000

Publisher, Patricia A. Pingry
Editor, Lisa C. Thompson
Art Director, Patrick McRae
Copy Editor, Michelle Prater Burke
Editorial Intern, Heather McArthur
Contributing Editors, Lansing Christman, Deana Deck, Russ Flint, Pamela Kennedy, Mary Skarmeas, Nancy Skarmeas

ACKNOWLEDGMENTS

THE WHITE OAK from *THE PASSING THRONG* by Edgar A. Guest, copyright 1923 by The Reilly & Lee Co., used by permission of the author's estate. APRIL RAIN SONG from THE DREAM KEEPER AND OTHER POEMS by Langston Hughes. Copyright 1932 by Alfred A. Knopf Inc. and renewed 1960 by Langston Hughes. Reprinted by permission of the publisher. WHENEVER I SEE LILACS BLOW from *ROSES IN DECEMBER* by Edna Jaques, published in Canada by Thomas Allen & Son Limited. Our sincere thanks to the following author whom we were unable to contact: Jonathan Henderson Brooks for THE RESURRECTION.

ATTENTION *IDEALS* READERS: The *Ideals* editors are looking for "favorite memories" to publish in the magazine. Please send a typed description of your favorite holiday memory or family tradition to: Favorite Memories, c/o Editorial Department, Ideals Publications Inc., P.O. Box 148000, Nashville, TN 37214-8000.

Daffodils

William Wordsworth

I wandered lonely as a cloud
That floats on high o'er vales and hills,
When all at once I saw a crowd—
A host of golden daffodils
Beside the lake, beneath the trees,
Fluttering and dancing in the breeze.

Continuous as the stars that shine
And twinkle on the Milky Way,
They stretch in never-ending line
Along the margin of a bay:
Ten thousand saw I, at a glance,
Tossing their heads in sprightly dance.

The waves beside them danced, but they
Outdid the sparkling waves in glee;
A poet could not be but gay
In such a jocund company;
I gazed—and gazed—but little thought
What wealth the show to me had brought.

For oft, when on my couch I lie,
In vacant or in pensive mood,
They flash upon that inward eye
Which is the bliss of solitude;
And then my heart with pleasure fills
And dances with the daffodils.